Sports Devos

100

for Girls

978-1-4336-8638-2

Published by B&H Publishing Group
Nashville, Tennessee
BHPublishingGroup.com

Custom edition published for LifeWay Christian Stores.

2 3 4 5 6 7 8 • 22 21 20 19 18

Sports Devos

100

for Girls

WRITTEN BY JOHN PATTON

B&H
KIDS
Nashville, Tennessee

Contents

Overcoming Fear

**For you did not receive a spirit of slavery
to fall back into fear, but you received the Spirit
of adoption, by whom we cry out, "*Abba*, Father."**

—Romans 8:15

There is nothing weak or wrong with being afraid. Sometimes being afraid to compete may make you wiser and stronger. Overcome fear by believing what God says about you and then walking one step at a time in the direction of belief in Him. You may "freeze" when shooting a free throw in the last second of the game and say to yourself, *I can't do this*. But know that no matter what, hit or miss, God still loves you.

When are you most afraid? How can God help you overcome your fears?

_____

_____

_____

_____

_____

_____

_____

_____

_____

_____

_____

_____

_____

_____

Playing with Fear

There is no fear in love; instead, perfect love drives out fear, because fear involves punishment. So the one who fears has not reached perfection in love.

—1 John 4:18

Has the fear of failure ever prevented you from competing in a sporting contest? Sometimes the fear of failure can keep you from giving your best effort on the field. You are afraid that if you fail, you will be laughed at, made fun of, scolded, embarrassed. Realize that God's love goes much deeper than any failure you may experience. He promises that He will never leave or forsake you, so even when the fear of failing hits you, you can continue to give your best effort and trust God for the rest.

Do you fear failure? What do you do when failure keeps you from trying?

_____

_____

_____

_____

_____

_____

_____

_____

_____

_____

_____

_____

_____

_____

Embarrassment

**In this, love is perfected with us so that
we may have confidence in the day of judgment,
for we are as He is in this world.**

—1 John 4:17

Have you ever lost a game by a really bad score? Most athletes at one time or another are going to be on a team in which they are going to get beaten really badly. As you walk across the court to shake hands, you feel ashamed. Realize that God loves you very much regardless of whether you win or lose. He is so proud of you for being a part of the team. Hold your head up and stand proud even in defeat, because God loves you regardless.

What gives you courage to keep your head up even when you lose the game?

_____

_____

_____

_____

_____

_____

_____

_____

_____

_____

_____

_____

_____

_____

_____

Attitude

**This is the day the Lord has made;
let us rejoice and be glad in it.**

—Psalm 118:24

What is your attitude when going into your practice or game? Realize that today is a gift from God. He has given you this day to live to the fullest and to enjoy Him and all He has created. He is the one who has given you the body, the mind, and the spirit to play your sport, so play to the best of your ability. Realize that today is the first day of the rest of your life and go for it with all the zest, passion, and strength you have. Enjoy this moment, for you can never relive this day.

What is your attitude when it's time for practice or time for your game? Are you having fun?

_____

_____

_____

_____

_____

_____

_____

_____

_____

_____

_____

_____

_____

_____

Mental Preparation

**You also be ready, because the Son of Man
is coming at an hour that you do not expect.**

—Luke 12:40

How important is it for you to be prepared and ready to face your opponent? As you grow older, mental preparation becomes as important as physical preparation. In basketball, coaches and players watch film to study the strengths and weaknesses of the opponents. Preparing for every scenario that might happen plays a big part in the game. Spend some time thinking about the game before the game begins. Then you will be ready when the time comes to give your best.

How do you get prepared for your next opponent? What helps you do your best?

_____

_____

_____

_____

_____

_____

_____

_____

_____

_____

_____

_____

_____

_____

_____

Trusting in God

**Pay attention to the sound of my cry,
my King and my God, for I pray to You.**

—Psalm 5:2

Have you ever felt all alone in your athletic contest? Some sports like tennis and golf are played individually. Feeling alone can be a scary thing, especially if you feel like you cannot meet the expectations laid out before you. Even before the game starts, pray. Pray for strength to play your hardest. Pray for your mind to be engaged fully. Pray for God to be with you every step of the way and know that He promises to never leave you or forsake you.

Is prayer a part of your preparation? What should you pray for? Who should you pray for?

_____

_____

_____

_____

_____

_____

_____

_____

_____

_____

_____

_____

Overcoming Nervousness

**You will keep the mind that is dependent on You
in perfect peace, for it is trusting in You.**

—Isaiah 26:3

Do you ever get nervous before your game and allow fear to rule your thoughts? Give your anxiety and fears to God. Tell Him why you are nervous and anxious. Tell Him why you are scared. The last part of this verse tells you why you can be content when you are preparing for your game—because we can trust in God. We can trust in God and believe that our success or failure does not define who we are. Be at peace and enjoy the moment.

How do you overcome anxiety or fear before your game? If you don't get nervous, how can you help others who do?

_____

_____

_____

_____

_____

_____

_____

_____

_____

_____

_____

_____

_____

_____

Playing in Defeat

**God, You know my foolishness, and my
guilty acts are not hidden from You.**

—Psalm 69:5

Have you ever missed a free throw in the last seconds of
the game to lose the game? If you play sports long enough,
there will be games you play great and games you play
lousy. When you miss a free throw, you feel like a failure.
God sees your missed free throws, your dropped passes,
your missed assignments, your penalties. Yet it does not
affect how He loves you at all. Your failures do not define
how God sees you. He loves you with an unconditional
love, meaning He loves you even when you fail. So, you
are free to play as hard as you can because failure does
not define you.

When you have missed an opportunity that cost you or your team the game, how do you react?

_____

_____

_____

_____

_____

_____

_____

_____

_____

_____

_____

_____

_____

Be Wise

**Pay careful attention, then, to how you walk—
not as unwise people but as wise.**

—Ephesians 5:15

In soccer, if your team has the lead late in the game, a wise coach may adjust the team strategy and have more players on defense than on offense. Her strategy is "we have the lead, so all we have to do to win the game is prevent them from scoring." It is a wise decision for the coach to do this at the right time and makes it hard for the opponent to beat them. Think about how you can be wise as you play your event. God has given you a mind as well as a body, so using your mind can play as big a part in winning as your physical body.

What are some ways you can use your mind to give your-self an advantage in the game?

_____

_____

_____

_____

_____

_____

_____

_____

_____

_____

_____

_____

_____

_____

Confidence in God

For You are my hope, Lord God**,
my confidence from my youth.**

—Psalm 71:5

In basketball, you must have confidence in your shot and believe it will go in when you take the shot. Your mental attitude is as important as the physical aspect of the game. If you think you won't make the shot, it is very rare that you will hit the shot. Have confidence in your shot. But also have confidence in God. He has given you your athletic ability, and He will be there for you every day of your life. Put your trust in Him and enjoy the game.

Are you confident? What does it mean to have confidence in your ability at your position?

_____

_____

_____

_____

_____

_____

_____

_____

_____

_____

_____

_____

_____

_____

_____

Give Thanks After the Game

But thanks be to God, who always puts us on display in Christ and through us spreads the aroma of the knowledge of Him in every place.

—2 Corinthians 2:14

When the game is over, do you make a line and shake hands with the opponents? You quickly say, "Good game," and repeat it to every one of their teammates. This is a great "routine" that goes on after the game because it shows you that it is just a game and your opponents are young women just like you. Both teams learn to give thanks to God for the opportunity to play the game and hopefully realize that it is just a game, and the way we treat one another is far more important than who may win or who may lose.

What happens after the game when your team wins? What happens when your team loses?

_____

_____

_____

_____

_____

_____

_____

_____

_____

_____

_____

_____

_____

_____

_____

_____

_____

Giving God Glory

**All You have made will thank You, Lord;
the godly will praise You.**

—Psalm 145:10

Do you think you can praise God by the way you play a game? When we think of praising God, we usually think of words we say with our mouth. But we also have the opportunity to praise God by the way we play. Sometimes you see an athlete stop briefly after something great has happened, like scoring a goal in soccer or hitting a great spike in volleyball, and quickly look up to the sky to give God glory for what just happened. She is pointing to God, giving Him glory for what she just did and thanking Him for the body to be able to compete in her sport.

When you are playing the game, how do you include God? How do you praise Him?

_____

_____

_____

_____

_____

_____

_____

_____

_____

_____

_____

_____

_____

_____

_____

Don't Compare Yourself to Others

But each person should examine his own work, and then he will have a reason for boasting in himself alone, and not in respect to someone else.

—Galatians 6:4

In cross-country or track every athlete has her own "PR." PR stands for "personal record." So every time she races, she is really competing not against the opponent, but against herself. She is trying to beat her own personal record. God has made each one of us uniquely different. Some of us can excel in some things while others excel in something else. All God asks you to do is give your best effort. Sometimes it may be good enough to win the event; sometimes it may not. Enjoy simply giving your best.

What are some things you do well? What are some things you don't do well?

_____

_____

_____

_____

_____

_____

_____

_____

_____

_____

_____

_____

_____

_____

Carry Your Burden

For each person will have to carry his own load.

—Galatians 6:5

In volleyball, each girl has her specific responsibility to cover to make the team successful. Between each hit, every member of the team has to adjust her position to make sure the court is fully covered. When one girl doesn't do her job and cover her responsibility, it leaves a gap or hole and makes it easy for the opponent to score. A big part of being on a team is learning what your load is (what the coach expects of you) and then doing that assignment to the best of your ability. The beauty of being a part of a team is realizing that you cannot do the task on your own, that you need each other. It's good to realize that you have a specific responsibility to help the team be stronger.

What are the specific responsibilities of people on your team? Do you work well together?

_____

_____

_____

_____

_____

_____

_____

_____

_____

_____

_____

_____

_____

_____

_____

God's Anchor for Us, His Love

We have this hope as an anchor for our lives, safe and secure. It enters the inner sanctuary behind the curtain.

—Hebrews 6:19

When you have a 3-2 count as a pitcher in softball, you want to throw the pitch you have the most confidence will hit the strike zone. You fall back on the thing you do the best and know you can do well. Spiritually, when you start doubting things in life, fall back on the anchor of God's unfailing and unconditional love. He will never fail you and will be there to the end.

Have you committed yourself to the unfailing anchor? How do you access God's love?

_____

_____

_____

_____

_____

_____

_____

_____

_____

_____

_____

_____

_____

_____

Examine Your Work

**Let us search out and examine our ways,
and then turn back to the Lord.**

—Lamentations 3:40

In school, teachers give tests to see what you have learned. The purpose for a test is for the teacher to see what material the students have learned and what material he may need to reteach. In sports, games can be like tests in school. They are a great way to see if you have learned what the coach has taught you. In basketball when the coach has you run a play, they are trusting that you have learned the offense and will execute the play the way they have drawn it up.

What are the hardest things to learn in your sport? How can God help you?

_____

_____

_____

_____

_____

_____

_____

_____

_____

_____

_____

_____

_____

_____

God Is Our Stronghold

The LORD is good, a stronghold in a day of distress;
He cares for those who take refuge in Him.

—Nahum 1:7

In close competition, there are times when the lead switches and each team is on top. When you get behind, it can be very easy to get your head down and not play quite as hard as you have been playing when you had the lead. But remember that God is there with you through thick and thin, through the times when you are winning and the times when you may fall behind. Keep your eyes on Him through the ups and downs of sports.

How do you feel when your team gets behind? What do you do to encourage others?

_____

_____

_____

_____

_____

_____

_____

_____

_____

_____

_____

_____

_____

_____

Strive for Peace with Your Opponent

**Pursue peace with everyone, and holiness—
without it no one will see the Lord.**

—Hebrews 12:14

What is your attitude toward your opponent? Do you have a hatred toward her and want to beat her as bad as you can? Or do you see her as a human being just like you, made in God's image? Your opponent is not your enemy. You are playing a game; it's not war. Treat your opponent the same way you would want to be treated. This does not mean you have to let her win. You play as hard as you can play and defeat her if you can, but realize that in the end it is just a game. Relationships are much more important.

What is your attitude toward your opponent? How do you like to be treated by the other team?

_____

_____

_____

_____

_____

_____

_____

_____

_____

_____

_____

_____

_____

_____

Don't Give Up

**We are pressured in every way but not crushed;
we are perplexed but not in despair.**

—2 Corinthians 4:8

"It ain't over until it is over." In basketball, a turnover can change the momentum of a game. The team that looked in control and had the game won can suddenly have something happen and be losing. When bad things happen in your game, learn how to play through the bad things and make them better. When someone fouls, encourage her and tell her to keep on going. Don't give up. More importantly, in life don't give up. There will be rainy days and sunny days. Thank the Lord for each and count it a blessing to be alive for another day.

What causes you to get discouraged? What do you do when bad things happen?

_____

_____

_____

_____

_____

_____

_____

_____

_____

_____

_____

_____

_____

God's Standard for Success

**Do not be conformed to this age,
but be transformed by the renewing of your mind.**

—Romans 12:2

How does the world view success? The world has only one person or team who is successful—the team that wins the championship. But God's view of success is much different. His view of success is for you to play your sport with all your heart, soul, mind, and strength. Sometimes this will result in victory in the world's eyes; but sometimes it may not. Play with all the passion and gusto you can, but keep the game in perspective. There will be other games on other days for you to play, so enjoy the moment.

Are you playing with all your heart, soul, mind, and strength? How do you view success?

_____

_____

_____

_____

_____

_____

_____

_____

_____

_____

_____

_____

_____

_____

Giving Thanks in All Things

Give thanks to Yahweh; call on His name; proclaim His deeds among the peoples.

—1 Chronicles 16:8

What are you thankful for? In this passage, King David is giving thanks to God for the ark of the covenant being brought back to Jerusalem. Think about your life and all you have to be thankful for, and give thanks. The last part of the verse tells us to give thanks to the people, to our families and our teammates. Encourage your teammates today by simply going up to them and telling them how thankful you are to be on the team with them, and watch them smile.

Do you have an attitude of gratitude? What are you thankful for? Who are you thankful for?

_____

_____

_____

_____

_____

_____

_____

_____

_____

_____

_____

_____

_____

_____

Reaching Forward

But one thing I do: Forgetting what is behind and reaching forward to what is ahead.

—Philippians 3:13

How do you respond when you make a mistake or fail? Every athlete who has ever played has made a mistake, has dropped a pass, has missed a shot at the goal, has missed a free throw, has made a bad set or missed a spike, and has struck out. But how you respond when you fail is crucial to how successful you can be as an athlete. Don't dwell on the past and let it get you down, rather focus on the "now" and look ahead. The "now" is what matters; what you are doing this play and this moment. Be totally focused on giving your all at this moment and keep going to the next moment.

How do you respond when you mess up? How do you feel about others when they mess up?

_____

_____

_____

_____

_____

_____

_____

_____

_____

_____

_____

_____

_____

_____

How God Defines Success

But seek first the kingdom of God and His righteousness, and all these things will be provided for you.

—Matthew 6:33

What does true success really look like? The world defines success by looking on the scoreboard. If you are ahead, you are a winner. If you are behind, you are a loser. But God defines success on a totally different scoreboard. In 1905 Bessie Stanley defined success as this: "He has achieved success who has lived well, laughed often and loved much." The scoreboard definition of success is only the surface. True success goes much deeper than simply what a scoreboard says. True success starts with valuing the things that God values, not what the world values.

How do you measure success? In what areas of your life are you successful?

_____

_____

_____

_____

_____

_____

_____

_____

_____

_____

_____

_____

_____

_____

_____

True Success

**Keep your obligation to the Lᴏʀᴅ your God . . .
so that you will have success in everything
you do and wherever you turn.**

—1 Kings 2:3

There is much more to a game than just winning. Sports has the great opportunity to build character in you and help develop you into a man. Sports can also tempt you in negative ways. We have seen many professional athletes whose lives have been destroyed by all the success they have had. The success tells them they can have anything they want, which is not true. When you are successful, realize that every step you take and every breath you take is because God has given you that precious gift. Realize that true success is keeping your eyes on Jesus.

Does being humble play a role in being a good athlete? How do you demonstrate humility when you win?

_____

_____

_____

_____

_____

_____

_____

_____

_____

_____

_____

_____

_____

_____

Boast in God

But the one who boasts should boast in this, that he understands and knows Me—that I am Yahweh, showing faithful love, justice, and righteousness on the earth, for I delight in these things. This is the Lord's declaration.

—Jeremiah 9:24

When you win a big game, how do you handle it? Do you boast in your win and taunt your opponents? Do you win arrogantly or do you win humbly? Enjoy the victory, but also realize that it is just a game and know that all you have is a gift from God. God is the one who has given you your body, your hands to throw and catch, your feet to run fast and strong, your mind to concentrate on the task at hand. Every part of your body is a gift from Him, so realize it is all a gift and play with thankfulness for that precious gift called life.

How do you handle winning? What does your opponent think about you when you win?

_____

_____

_____

_____

_____

_____

_____

_____

_____

_____

_____

_____

_____

_____

Character

He stores up success for the upright;
He is a shield for those who live with integrity.

—Proverbs 2:7

Who are you when no one is looking? Sometimes a coach will tell you to do a certain workout and trust that you will do all the repetitions on your own. If she tells you to do ten sit ups, it is easy to do nine without anyone knowing. But being true and honest in even little things like sit ups will develop your character. Character is doing the right thing even when no one else is looking. Strive to be a man of character who is honest and truthful to your family and friends. Be someone who your friends can come to when they need a friend who will help them choose the right path.

Who are you when no one is looking? Where do you need to work on honesty and truthfulness?

_____

_____

_____

_____

_____

_____

_____

_____

_____

_____

_____

_____

_____

_____

_____

_____

Rejoice with Your Teammates

Everyone should look out not only for his own interests, but also for the interests of others.

—Philippians 2:4

How do you respond when your teammate gets success and you don't? The beauty of a team sport is that it takes more than just one person to be successful. It takes all of you; and there will be times when others on the team get honors and awards that you want or desire. Take the eyes off of yourself and look to your teammates. Rejoice with them when they get pats on the back. Hurt with them when they mess up. Being on a team means there are many of you who make up the "team." Notice your teammates and be able to recognize their success when it comes.

How do you respond when your teammate gets success and you don't? Are you sincerely happy for her?

_____

_____

_____

_____

_____

_____

_____

_____

_____

_____

_____

_____

_____

_____

_____

A Good Reputation

**A good name is to be chosen over great wealth;
favor is better than silver and gold.**

—Proverbs 22:1

How will your teammates remember you? Believe it or not, they will remember you and you will remember them. What they will remember about you is how you treated them as a person. Did you respect them? Did you encourage them? Did you rejoice with them when they had success? Did you console them when they had failure? They will also remember your work ethic during practice and games. Did you give all you had in practice and games and never give up? The things that truly matter are not the things that are seen (like the scoreboard), but rather the unseen things like your character and integrity.

How will your teammates remember you? What kind of reputation do you have?

_____

_____

_____

_____

_____

_____

_____

_____

_____

_____

_____

_____

_____

_____

Treat Opponents with Respect

Act wisely toward outsiders, making the most of the time. Your speech should always be gracious, seasoned with salt, so that you may know how you should answer each person.

—Colossians 4:5–6

What do you say to your opponents? When you watch professional sports, it is easy to see a lot of "trash talk" when opponents speak to one another? Trash talk is telling the opponent how much better you are. But the Bible challenges us to treat our opponents with great respect and honor. This doesn't mean you let up in your performance. You still play as hard as you can and strive to win, but also realize your opponent is a human being just like you and treat her as such. If the opportunity presents itself pat her on the back and say, "Good job."

Do you do a lot of "trash talking"? How do you react when it comes from your opponent?

_____

_____

_____

_____

_____

_____

_____

_____

_____

_____

_____

_____

_____

_____

Be an Encourager

**Joseph, a Levite and a Cypriot by birth,
the one the apostles called Barnabas,
which is translated Son of Encouragement.**

—Acts 4:36

In the Bible, about all we know of a man named Barnabas is that his name means "son of encouragement." He was known simply because he encouraged others. Anyone can encourage others. You don't have to be the best athlete on the team or the worst, but the opportunity to encourage your teammates is available for everyone. Think about how much it builds you up when someone else says something good to you. Do the same for them. Be an encourager to your teammates. Never underestimate the power of encouraging words to your teammates.

Are you known as an encourager? How has someone encouraged you?

_____

_____

_____

_____

_____

_____

_____

_____

_____

_____

_____

_____

_____

_____

God's Feedback

**Search me, God, and know my heart;
test me and know my concerns.**

—Psalm 139:23

How do you respond when others give you feedback about your performance? Their words can either crush you or build you up. But what about feedback from God? In your prayer time, ask God for feedback. There are many ways He can speak to you. He may speak through your parents, your siblings, your friends, or your coach. Or He may just speak to you through your own conscience. His evaluation of you is so valuable because He sees you as you truly are and will encourage you accordingly. He sees you as a daughter and will encourage you with words that will make you a better athlete and a better person.

How do you respond when others give you feedback about your performance? Have you asked God for feedback?

_____

_____

_____

_____

_____

_____

_____

_____

_____

_____

_____

_____

_____

_____

_____

_____

Put Relationship Above Things

The one who loves a pure heart and gracious lips—the king is his friend.

—Proverbs 22:11

What is more important, the relationships you have with your teammates or the trophy you may receive for being on the team? Hopefully you realize that the relationships you develop on your team are more important than any prize you may receive for being on the team. We all long to be loved. We want to have friends. When we learn to speak to one another with pure, gracious, honest speech, we will find that we have friends as a result. Before going to practice today, think of what you can say or which of your teammates may need some words of encouragement, and be that friend for her.

What's more important: winning or relationships? How does winning or losing change your team?

_____

_____

_____

_____

_____

_____

_____

_____

_____

_____

_____

_____

_____

_____

_____

_____

Give Thanks in All Things

Rejoice always! Pray constantly. Give thanks in everything, for this is God's will for you in Christ Jesus.

—1 Thessalonians 5:16–18

Are you able to give thanks even when you lose? It is easy to give thanks when we win or when we do well, but much more difficult to do so when we lose or perform poorly. This Scripture tells us to give thanks in all circumstances, even when we lose. Why or how should we give thanks when we lose or perform poorly? Because life is about relationships, not performance. Even in a lose or poor performance we have the opportunity to build relationships with others. A loss is an opportunity to build character in you, so you see that you can grow through "all things."

Are you thankful when you lose? How should you react when you lose? Does a loss define who you are?

_____

_____

_____

_____

_____

_____

_____

_____

_____

_____

_____

_____

_____

_____

Strive for Excellence

And I pray this: that your love will keep on growing in knowledge and every kind of discernment, so that you can approve the things that are superior and can be pure and blameless in the day of Christ.

—Philippians 1:9–10

Do you strive for excellence in your sport? Do you strive to be the best you can be? Most athletes set goals and push themselves to achieve those goals. You may set a goal to shoot 100 free throws a day, and set a goal of making 80 percent of them. Once you achieve that goal on a regular basis, you set higher goals. Achieving excellence is about planning, preparing, and performing. Set realistic high goals and strive to be the best you can be.

Do you strive to be the best you can be? What goals have you set? Have you achieved them?

_____

_____

_____

_____

_____

_____

_____

_____

_____

_____

_____

_____

_____

_____

_____

Bear One Another's Burdens

**Carry one another's burdens;
in this way you will fulfill the law of Christ.**

—Galatians 6:2

Do you care about your teammates? Does it matter to you if they succeed or fail? Does it hurt you if they get hurt? In life it is very easy to get caught up into "you" and not notice or even care about those around you. But life is not meant to be lived just pleasing yourself and your own interests. It is made to be in relationship with others. Sports is one of the greatest ways to learn how to care about others. Today, notice your teammates. See if you can see which ones may be hurting and which ones may be happy. Enter into their lives and you will find your life is much richer as a result.

How do members of your team care for each other? Do you know their names and how they're doing?

_____

_____

_____

_____

_____

_____

_____

_____

_____

_____

_____

_____

_____

_____

Mentorship

**And what you have heard from me in the presence
of many witnesses, commit to faithful men
who will be able to teach others also.**

—2 Timothy 2:2

Do you have a hero, a role model? Is there someone that you hope to be like one day? Is your answer to the questions above a professional athlete or is it someone you know personally, like your mother or your coach? Try to think of women older than you that you know who you admire. Watch the way they handle themselves when they are playing and when they are off the court. If you have the chance, ask them if they can mentor or train you. The lessons you can gain from that mentorship will be very valuable lessons in life.

Who is your role model? Who do you hope to be like one day and why?

_____

_____

_____

_____

_____

_____

_____

_____

_____

_____

_____

_____

_____

_____

Being on a Team

**If then there is any encouragement in Christ,
if any consolation of love, if any fellowship with
the Spirit, if any affection and mercy, fulfill my
joy by thinking the same way, having the same love,
sharing the same feelings, focusing on one goal.**

—Philippians 2:1–2

What can you learn from being part of a team? This verse lists several things that being on a team can give you. Encouragement—learn how to give and receive encouraging words to build each other up. Love—learn how to love your teammates and truly care for them. Talk with them outside of practice and learn what is important to them outside of sports. Affection and sympathy—learn how to rejoice with other's success and hurt with other's pain.

What can you learn from your team? How does being on the team change your life?

_____

_____

_____

_____

_____

_____

_____

_____

_____

_____

_____

_____

_____

_____

Steadfastness

Consider it a great joy, my bothers, whenever you experience various trials, knowing that the testing of your faith produces endurance.

—James 1:2–3

What is steadfastness and how do sports teach us steadfastness? Steadfastness is the ability to keep on trying and trying even when it seems pointless and you can't succeed. In a game, steadfastness keeps putting pressure on the opponent play after play. In practice, it is practicing a play time and time again. You repeat the play so many times you think you can do it in your sleep. Then when you are in a game and the pressure is on, you fall back to those practiced plays when you did it over and over again. Your steadfastness pushes you through the difficult times in a game and more importantly in life.

What is your attitude toward things that you have to do over and over again?

_____

_____

_____

_____

_____

_____

_____

_____

_____

_____

_____

_____

_____

_____

Physical Training

"Even so, be strong, Zerubbabel"—this is the LORD's
declaration. "Be strong, Joshua son of Jehozadak,
high priest. Be strong, all you people of the
land"—this is the LORD's declaration. "Work! For
I am with you"—the declaration of the LORD of Hosts.

—Haggai 2:4

How important is it for you to be as strong as you can be
for your team? Your teammates are counting on you to
work hard not just on game day but in practice as well.
Sometimes training workouts don't seem like they matter.
If you do all the push ups and sit ups you can, you don't
notice the difference immediately. When it will show up
is late in a game when your team needs you to give a little
extra effort to score, and your body has been trained to
push itself to make the goal.

How important is it for you to be as strong as you can be for your team?

_____

_____

_____

_____

_____

_____

_____

_____

_____

_____

_____

_____

_____

_____

God's Strength

Then Job replied to the LORD: I know that You can do anything and no plan of Yours can be thwarted.

—Job 42:1–2

Do you pray to God to give you strength? In the Bible, the book of Job talks about how Job had to learn the lesson that God is in control and will give you strength to face the task before you. Sometimes you just need to pray for strength to make it through the day. You didn't get enough sleep the night before and are tired. Sometimes you need strength to make it through the next play. Pray for strength, especially in games and practices. God is willing and able to grant your request.

How does God answer your prayers? Can you tell a difference when you pray?

_____

_____

_____

_____

_____

_____

_____

_____

_____

_____

_____

_____

_____

_____

Confidence in God

For we have become companies of the Messiah if we hold firmly until the end of reality that we had at the start.

—Hebrews 3:14

How important is it for you to have confidence in the fourth quarter that your offense can score or your defense can stop your opponent? Crucial! If you don't believe you can succeed, there is a very slim chance that you will succeed. You practice and practice until you know the play by heart, by instinct. Then in the heat of the game when you need to execute it perfectly, you can because you have practiced it and because you have confidence it will work. Also have confidence and trust that God who has been faithful in the past will continue to be faithful today and tomorrow.

Do you have confidence in God? How do you know you can trust Him to be there for you?

_____

_____

_____

_____

_____

_____

_____

_____

_____

_____

_____

_____

_____

_____

_____

Magnify God Together

**Proclaim Yahweh's greatness with me;
let us exalt His name together.**

—Psalm 34:3

Do you ever thank God for what He has done for you? This verse commands us to magnify or praise God together for what He has done for us. It is one thing for you to lift up and thank God individually, but what about your team? Depending on your situation, you may be able to do this with the coach leading you. But you may not be in a situation where you can lift God up as a team. Ask the coach if you can either pray or just say a quick word to the team and thank God for giving all of your teammates the ability and the opportunity to play the game.

Do you have a time every day to thank God for all that He has done for you? How do you plan for that time?

_____

_____

_____

_____

_____

_____

_____

_____

_____

_____

_____

_____

_____

Wake Up with Jesus

Very early in the morning, while it was still dark, He got up, went out, and made His way to a deserted place. And He was praying there.

—Mark 1:35

What is the first thing on your mind when you wake up? Maybe it is the game you have that day. Maybe it is the practice or workout you get to do that day. Jesus had a habit of spending time with the Father every day. When you wake and before the busyness of the day kicks in, try to spend some time just focusing on God and sharing with Him about your day. Tell Him what you are excited about, what you are scared of, what you like, what you don't like. Just share your heart with Him and know that He will be with you every step of your day.

What is the first thing on your mind when you wake up?
Does it include the Father?

_____

_____

_____

_____

_____

_____

_____

_____

_____

_____

_____

_____

_____

Give God Your Fears

**Do not fear, for I am with you; do not be afraid,
for I am your God. I will strengthen you; I will help you;
I will hold on to you with My righteous right hand.**

—Isaiah 41:10

In your sporting event, what scares you? Are you afraid of losing, failing, or getting hurt? Usually we each have our own fears that can paralyze us from trying if we let them take control of us. But we must remember that God promises to be here with us, to fight for us, to never leave or forsake us. Therefore we can overcome our fears and go for it in our sport. Give God your fears and feel the freedom to be able to give your all to your sport.

How do you know God is always with you? Have you told Him your fears?

_____

_____

_____

_____

_____

_____

_____

_____

_____

_____

_____

_____

_____

Live in Harmony with One Another

Finally, brothers, rejoice. Become mature, be encouraged, be of the same mind, be at peace, and the God of love and peace will be with you.

—2 Corinthians 13:11

It is really important how you treat your teammates and your opponents. Because sports are so intense, there will be times when you butt heads with your teammates and your opponents. The heat of the moment may make you say or do things you regret later. God challenges you to go back and try to make things right with them, to restore the broken relationship. He wants you to strive to live in harmony with one another, whether it be your teammate or your opponent. Remember the game is just a game, but the relationships you build on the team last much longer.

Have you gotten mad at your teammates? How did you work it out?

_____

_____

_____

_____

_____

_____

_____

_____

_____

_____

_____

_____

_____

_____

Worshipping God

**Therefore, since we are receiving a kingdom
that cannot be shaken, let us hold on to grace. By it,
we may serve God acceptably, with reverence and awe.**

—Hebrews 12:28

How can you worship God in your sport? Acceptable worship does not just happen when you go to church on a Sunday morning or Wednesday night. Worship can and should happen every day. You have the opportunity to worship God every day when you practice, every game you play. How? First of all by thanking Him for the ability He has given you to run around and move. Then run around and move with all your strength. Playing your sport all out is a form of worshipping God!

How can you worship God in your sport? Are there ways your team can pray and thank God together? How?

_____

_____

_____

_____

_____

_____

_____

_____

_____

_____

_____

_____

_____

_____

Give Thanks

**Let us enter His presence with thanksgiving;
let us shout triumphantly to Him in song.**

—Psalm 95:2

Why is it so important to give thanks to God for things? Because every thing you have comes as a gift from Him. Every breath you take is because He has given you another breath. Every step you take, every shot you shoot, every ball you kick, is because He has given you the ability to play your sport. So playing with everything you have with an attitude of thanksgiving develops in you an appreciation for the game and for each new day. Live your life with an attitude of thanksgiving, and you will be blessed.

Why is it so important to give thanks to God? What are some of the things you are thankful for?

_____

_____

_____

_____

_____

_____

_____

_____

_____

_____

_____

_____

_____

_____

_____

Enjoy Your Emotions

You who are now hungry are blessed, because you will be filled. You who now weep are blessed, because you will laugh.

—Luke 6:21

Think of the last time you cried. Was it because of pain, sadness, happiness, or sorrow? Sporting events bring out all sorts of emotions. In a given game, there can be a time for every emotion you have. One minute you may be sad because you had a turnover and the next minute you can be so happy because you or your teammates made a great play to overcome the sadness. Enjoy all the emotions you experience in playing sports and be thankful that one day Jesus will make all things new and overcome all our sadness.

What different emotions do you experience before, during, and after a game or practice?

_____

_____

_____

_____

_____

_____

_____

_____

_____

_____

_____

_____

_____

_____

_____

God Is Righteous

God is a righteous judge.

—Psalm 7:11

Have you ever had a judgment call go against you? Has the official ever made a bad call? How did you respond? There may be times that you respond negatively. You may lose your temper and yell back at him. He then has the power to give you a technical or throw you out of the game. Officials are human beings as well. They will make mistakes. Treat them with respect. Be thankful that God is a righteous judge who never makes a bad call. You can praise God for His justice.

What do you do when there's a bad call? How do your teammates react?

_____

_____

_____

_____

_____

_____

_____

_____

_____

_____

_____

_____

_____

_____

_____

_____

You Have Been Redeemed

**The Holy One of Israel is our Redeemer;
Yahweh of Hosts is His name.**

—Isaiah 47:4

Do you ever wish you could get another try at that last free throw or last kick? *Redeem* means to buy back that which was lost. Often times in sporting events you make mistakes. In basketball, a "foul" is a defensive or offensive mistake. But you get five fouls before you are taken out of the game. When you make a mistake, you can learn from it and then redeem yourself by making good plays that overcome the foul. Realize that in most sporting events you will get opportunities to "try again." Learn from your mistakes and then be prepared to try again. Also remember that God has redeemed you, bought you back, and made you His own son. Enjoy it.

Do you ever wish you could get another try at that last free throw or last kick? What can you do about it?

_____

_____

_____

_____

_____

_____

_____

_____

_____

_____

_____

_____

_____

_____

_____

Earnest Counsel

Oil and incense bring joy to the heart, and the sweetness of a friend is better than self-counsel.

—Proverbs 27:9

Do you build your teammates up or tear them down with your words and actions? Your words are very powerful. You have the opportunity with your words to tear your teammates down by negative talk. You can blame others for mistakes made. It is very easy to point the finger at others when things don't go right. Or you have the opportunity to bring earnest counsel to your friends. You have the opportunity to build them up with your words. When they make a mistake, you have the opportunity to be there for them to build them up and not tear them down. Be that friend who brings true and honest counsel to your teammates.

Do you build your teammates up or tear them down with your words and actions? What should you do?

_____

_____

_____

_____

_____

_____

_____

_____

_____

_____

_____

_____

_____

Winners and Losers

Instead, God has chosen what is foolish in the world to shame the wise, and God has chosen what is weak in the world to shame the strong.

—1 Corinthians 1:27

How does the world define success? By the scoreboard. According to the world, if you win on the scoreboard you win in life. God's scoreboard is not defined by winning or losing, but by what is inside your heart. According to the world, if you don't make the team or if you don't start, you are a loser. But God doesn't care if you make the team or if you start. He is more concerned about you giving all you have to give. If in giving all you have to give you make the team or you start or you even win, that is great. But that is not what defines you or what determines if you are a winner or not.

How do you feel when the scoreboard says you lost? Are you really a loser?

_____

_____

_____

_____

_____

_____

_____

_____

_____

_____

_____

_____

_____

_____

_____

Wisdom Is Learning from Others

**A wise son brings joy to his father,
but a foolish son, heartache to his mother.**

—Proverbs 10:1

Who is your biggest fan? Odds are it is your mother or your father. They are the ones who get you to the games and practices and cheer you on in your victories and your losses. A wise daughter is teachable, meaning she listens to her coach and does her best to obey her commands. A wise daughter is also one who listens to her mom and dad and learns from their instruction as well. A wise athlete is humble, meaning she knows that she can learn more about the game from those people around her who are older and have experience in the game that she hasn't gained yet and learn from their experience.

What is your attitude toward those who cheer for you or take you to the practices and games?

_____

_____

_____

_____

_____

_____

_____

_____

_____

_____

_____

_____

_____

_____

Thankful Heart

I always thank my God for you because of God's grace given to you in Christ Jesus, that by Him you were enriched in everything—in all speech and all knowledge.

—1 Corinthians 1:4–5

Do you have a thankful heart for all you have been given? You can look at others and wish you had their gifts or talents and become bitter that you don't have their gifts. Or you can take a step back, look at all He has given you, and realize that everything you have is a gift from God. Often you see athletes look up and point to God after a great play. They are quickly taking a brief second to thank God for the gifts they have received. Live your life with a thankful heart, and be blessed.

Do you have a thankful heart for all you have been given?
What gifts do you believe God has given you?

_____

_____

_____

_____

_____

_____

_____

_____

_____

_____

_____

_____

_____

_____

Rules Protect Us

I am Yahweh your God. Follow My statutes, keep My ordinances, and practice them.

—Ezekiel 20:19

Each game has rules that you must abide by. Why? Can you imagine playing a game where each player could make up her own rules? It would be crazy. Each player would only make up rules that would give the advantage to her. Yet that is not the way games are played. Games have rules and one of the reasons for the rules is to protect us. In soccer, running over a player is a penalty. Why? Such rules are made to protect players from getting hurt. In life, God has given us rules in the Bible. These rules are not to rob our joy but rather to protect us.

Can you imagine playing a game where each player could make up her own rules? What could happen?

_____

_____

_____

_____

_____

_____

_____

_____

_____

_____

_____

_____

_____

_____

_____

_____

What Is Your Role?

Samuel continued, "Although you once considered yourself unimportant, have you not become the leader of the tribes of Israel? The Lord anointed you king over Israel."

—1 Samuel 15:17

What is your role on the team? In basketball, a coach has to decide which five players will start. Each starter may have a specific role that he plays that makes the team stronger. One may be better at shooting against a zone defense whereas another may be better at driving against a man-to-man defense. Learn your role and do your best to fulfill your role. No matter what your role is, you are needed on the team to make your team the best it can be.

What is your role on the team? Have you had different roles, or do you want a different role?

_____

_____

_____

_____

_____

_____

_____

_____

_____

_____

_____

_____

_____

_____

Learning from Past Mistakes

**A wise man will listen and increase his learning,
and a discerning man will obtain guidance.**

—Proverbs 1:5

What can you learn from your past mistakes? As you get older, you may have the opportunity to watch films with your coach after a game. You may hear a saying: "The eye in the sky doesn't lie." What this means is the camera that films the game shows exactly what happened on each play. It will show you things you did very well and will also show you things you might need improving. A wise athlete will watch the eye in the sky and learn from his past mistakes. Learn how to be obedient and able to take constructive criticism.

What can you learn from your past mistakes? How have others helped you see where you need to change?

_____

_____

_____

_____

_____

_____

_____

_____

_____

_____

_____

_____

_____

_____

_____

Overcome the World

**Who is the one who conquers the world but the
one who believes in Jesus is the Son of God?**

—1 John 5:5

In sports, what does it take to overcome your opponent?
Often it takes more than just strength. Often it takes wisdom, experience, and preparation. For Christians we learn
to overcome the world by realizing who we have on our
team living inside us—Jesus. Because Jesus is on our
side and lives inside us, we can defeat the world no matter what it throws at us. Jesus who lives inside of you is
greater than the world. Believe it!

What does it take to overcome your opponent? To overcome at school or home?

_____

_____

_____

_____

_____

_____

_____

_____

_____

_____

_____

_____

_____

_____

Don't Lose Heart

Therefore, since we have this ministry because we were shown mercy, we do not give up.

—2 Corinthians 4:1

Have you ever had the urge to just give up in a game? If you are way behind and don't see any way you can win the game, your natural tendency is to just give up and stop trying. But if we are playing to honor and please God, He gives us the motivation and strength to give our all even when we may be way behind on the scoreboard. God's mercy toward us gives us the strength to keep going even when it is easy to lose heart and give up.

Do you give up when the game isn't going well? How do you fight your way through?

_____

_____

_____

_____

_____

_____

_____

_____

_____

_____

_____

_____

_____

Be an Example for Others

**Let no one despise your youth; instead,
you should be an example to the believers
in speech, in conduct, in love, in faith, in purity.**

—1 Timothy 4:12

Do you ever feel like you are just too young to really make a difference on your team or in someone's life? Don't believe it for a minute. You are never too young to start making a difference in your teammates lives. You have the opportunity to love and encourage them in such a way that it can change their lives. They see something in you that challenges them to be a better player, a better person. Encourage your teammates by what you say and how you treat them.

How can you make a difference on your team or in someone's life? Are you too young?

_____

_____

_____

_____

_____

_____

_____

_____

_____

_____

_____

_____

_____

_____

_____

Be a Difference Maker

**I know your works, that you are neither
cold nor hot. I wish that you were cold or hot.**

—Revelation 3:15

Don't settle for being mediocre when you can be better.
The world tells us that just existing is okay, that just being
satisfied with the middle of the road is fine. God wants
you to do so much more than simply exist. He wants you
to be passionate about whatever you do. Your talent level
may put you at the middle of the team or lower, but your
passion and desire should challenge your teammates to
be better players. Be passionate about what you do and
don't settle for just being there on the team. Be a difference maker.

Do you make a difference on your team? How is your attitude helping your team improve?

_____

_____

_____

_____

_____

_____

_____

_____

_____

_____

_____

_____

_____

_____

_____

Freely You Have Received; Freely Give

**Whatever your hands find to do,
do with all your strength.**

—Ecclesiastes 9:10

How much does it cost for you to go to practice or play in a game? Your parents probably had to pay a fee to join the team or league. Think about what God has given you as an athlete—the physical ability to play and parents and coaches who care enough about you to put you on this team. So whether you realize it or not, you have received a huge gift by being able to play. Once you realize this, you can then give back to your parents and the team by giving your all at every practice and every game.

How has your family had to sacrifice for you to be on the team? What has your coach's family had to sacrifice?

_____

_____

_____

_____

_____

_____

_____

_____

_____

_____

_____

_____

_____

_____

Be Silent and Learn to Listen

**But the Lord is in His holy temple;
let everyone on earth be silent in His presence.**

—Habakkuk 2:20

How hard is it for you to be silent for a short time? Silence is a very good thing and in our world it is sometimes very hard to find places where you can experience silence. Before games, coaches often want their players to be silent and to mentally think about what their job is in the game. Usually players will even fill up their silence with music, more noise. Take the challenge to just be quiet and listen to the silence. God often speaks the loudest when we still ourselves enough to hear Him.

How hard is it for you to be silent for a short time? When did you speak when you should have been silent?

_____

_____

_____

_____

_____

_____

_____

_____

_____

_____

_____

_____

_____

_____

_____

God Honors Humility

He raises the poor from the dust and lifts the needy from the garbage pile. He seats them with noblemen and gives them a throne of honor. For the foundations of the earth are the LORD's; He has set the world on them.

—1 Samuel 2:8

What God honors and lifts up is so different from what the world honors. The world honors the one who succeeds on the scoreboard. God honors the lowly and humble in heart. The lowly and humble in heart are not just the "losers." They are those who know that everything they have is a gift from God and therefore play each play in a spirit of humility. They are honored for the way they treat their coaches, their teammates, and even their opponents.

Does your attitude reflect humility and thankfulness? What are ways you feel God has honored you?

_____

_____

_____

_____

_____

_____

_____

_____

_____

_____

_____

_____

_____

_____

Breaking Bad Habits

**Therefore, put to death what
belongs to your worldly nature.**

—Colossians 3:5

Do you have some bad habits that you are trying to break? Usually when a young girl is learning how to shoot a basketball, she will develop poor form simply because it takes so much strength to get the ball to the goal. As she becomes stronger, she realizes that she has developed poor form and needs to break her bad habits to become a better player. Overcoming bad habits takes discipline and training time and time again. You have heard the statement, "Practice makes perfect." Practice is also a way to overcome a bad habit that may be hindering your performance.

Do you have some bad habits you are trying to break? How have others helped you recognize those habits?

_____

_____

_____

_____

_____

_____

_____

_____

_____

_____

_____

_____

_____

_____

Fear the Lord

Then Peter began to speak: "Now I really understand that God doesn't show favoritism, but in every nation the person who fears Him and does righteousness is acceptable to Him."

—Acts 10:34–35

What does it mean to fear the Lord? Fear in an athletic world is seen as a negative thing. "You can't be afraid and you must face your fears" is what we hear. But a fear of the Lord is a very good thing. To fear God is to have an awe and respect for Him. It does not drive you farther away from Him; rather it drives you closer to Him with humility and respect. You realize His power and strength, and you worship Him in all you do.

What does it mean to fear the Lord? What causes you to be closer to Him?

_____

_____

_____

_____

_____

_____

_____

_____

_____

_____

_____

_____

_____

_____

A Team of Love

**From Him the whole body, fitted and knit together
by every supporting ligament, promotes the growth
of the body for building up itself in love by
the proper working of each individual part.**

—Ephesians 4:16

A team is like a body. Each part of the body has a specific role and job to do to make the body work to perfection. When you sprint, think of how many body parts are involved and how crucial it is for each part to do its job perfectly. If for one step the leg says, "I don't want to be a leg anymore. I want to be an arm," it will mess up the whole body. But as a team, each person must do their job so the team is built up in love. A loving team is one where every member does his job for the good of the team.

How do your team members relate to each other? Is there bitterness and grumbling or kindness and love?

_____

_____

_____

_____

_____

_____

_____

_____

_____

_____

_____

_____

_____

_____

_____

Feel Your Emotions

**There is an occasion for everything,
and a time for every activity under heaven.**

—Ecclesiastes 3:1

What emotion are you feeling right now? Are you happy, sad, mad, afraid, or worried? God is the God of emotion. He is the one who gives us emotions as we go through life. In sports, there will be times when you experience all of these emotions. You are happy when you win, sad when you lose. You will be mad when you feel like an official made a bad call. You may face some opponents who simply scare you. You may be worried when you or a teammate get hurt. Don't deny these emotions. Feel them and thank God for creating you in a way that you can experience emotions.

Have you experienced a variety of emotions because you play on a team? Are you free to express those?

_____

_____

_____

_____

_____

_____

_____

_____

_____

_____

_____

_____

_____

_____

_____

Treat One Another Fairly

**But you, why do you criticize your brother?
Or you, why do you look down on your brother?
For we will all stand before the tribunal of God.**

—Romans 14:10

Do you cut down or build up your teammates? Anyone can criticize and cut down others, but it takes someone special to keep his mouth closed and refrain from saying bad things about another person, regardless of it being a teammate or opponent. Before you speak, think about what you are going to say. If the words are negative and tearing others down, don't say them. If they are encouraging and build up others, speak up. Remember God is the judge of all. He knows each and every one of us and knows the motives of our hearts.

Do you cut down or build up your teammates? How can you encourage the people around you?

_____

_____

_____

_____

_____

_____

_____

_____

_____

_____

_____

_____

_____

Learn from Others and Allow Others to Learn from You

Joshua son of Nun was filled with the spirit of wisdom because Moses had laid his hands on him. So the Israelites obeyed him and did as the Lord had commanded Moses.

—Deuteronomy 34:9

Who are you training to be a better athlete? Even at a young age, you have the opportunity to be a positive example for others. Joshua sat at Moses feet and observed him lead the people of Israel for at least forty years. Then when it came time for him to lead, he was well prepared and ready for the opportunity. Learn from others. Observe the way they play, the way they treat others. Then when it is your turn, be a positive example for others to learn from you.

Who are you training to be a better athlete? How are you sharing your skills with others?

_____

_____

_____

_____

_____

_____

_____

_____

_____

_____

_____

_____

_____

Give God Your Nervousness

Don't worry about anything, but in everything, through prayer and petition with thanksgiving, let your requests be made known to God. And the peace of God, which surpasses every thought, will guard your hearts and minds in Christ Jesus.

—Philippians 4:6–7

Do you get nervous before a game? In sporting events, getting nervous before a game is usually a good sign. It means you are thinking about what you need to do and how you need to perform. The Bible challenges you to give your nervousness to the Lord. Tell Him that you are nervous and even scared about your opponent. When you do this, a neat thing happens. God fills you with peace. He seems to whisper to you that you are okay and no matter what happens He will be there for you. It frees you up to give all you have to give for Him and your team.

Do you get nervous before a game? If you do, how can God help you?

_____

_____

_____

_____

_____

_____

_____

_____

_____

_____

_____

_____

_____

God Is with You

**Do not fear, for I am with you;
I will bring your descendants from the east,
and gather you from the west.**

—Isaiah 43:5

Do you ever get scared to face your challenge? Sometimes you will have to face opponents who are much bigger, stronger, faster, and even better than you. How can you do it? How can you give your best when you face superior opponents? Remember from Scripture it says time and time again that God will never leave you. He will be with you every step of the way. He will protect you and will never leave you or forsake you. He will give you the strength to face superior opponents.

How can you give your best when you face superior opponents? What is the first thing you should do to be ready?

_____

_____

_____

_____

_____

_____

_____

_____

_____

_____

_____

_____

_____

Be Self-Controlled

For this very reason, make every effort to supplement your faith with goodness, goodness with knowledge, knowledge with self-control, self-control with endurance, endurance with godliness, godliness with brotherly affection, and brotherly affection with love.

—2 Peter 1:5–7

How easy is it for you to lose your temper during the game? In each sport, players are penalized when they lose control and burst out in anger, as they should be. But God calls us to be self-controlled, to be able to hold back our anger and not display it in a negative way. When you get angry, try to step back and realize what it is that made you so mad. If you can do something about it, confront the issue calmly and in control. If you just need to let it go, then let it go and move on to the next play.

How easy is it for you to lose your temper during the game? How do you maintain self-control?

_____

_____

_____

_____

_____

_____

_____

_____

_____

_____

_____

_____

_____

_____

Be Persistent in Doing the Right Thing

So Jotham strengthened himself because he did not waver in obeying the LORD his God.

—2 Chronicles 27:6

Do what is right day after day. King Jotham grew powerful because he consistently sought the Lord day in and day out. He was a great king because he remained faithful to the Lord day by day. As an athlete, keep persistent in your practice day after day. When the coach tells you to do ten laps, do ten laps, not nine. When she tells you to touch the line, touch the line every time. Push yourself when you are tired and keep faithful to do what the coach tells you.

Do you do what's right every day? What things tempt you to cut corners or just do a little less?

_____

_____

_____

_____

_____

_____

_____

_____

_____

_____

_____

_____

_____

_____

Be Thankful for Jesus

**But thanks be to God, who gives us the
victory through our Lord Jesus Christ.**

—1 Corinthians 15:57

What are you thankful for today? The neat thing about
being thankful is that it may change every day. Something
will happen today and leave you the opportunity to be
thankful for something in your life. A thankful heart realizes that every gift comes from the Lord, the giver of all.
The victory He gives us in Jesus Christ is greater than any
sporting event victory we will ever experience. For that
we can be very thankful.

What are you thankful for today? Make a list and add to it when you remember something else.

_____

_____

_____

_____

_____

_____

_____

_____

_____

_____

_____

_____

_____

_____

Sow Good Seed

**In the morning sow your seed, and at evening
do not let your hand rest, because you don't know
which will succeed, whether one or the other,
or if both of them will be equally good.**

—Ecclesiastes 11:6

Do you ever get tired and weary of practicing over and over again? Don't lose heart. A farmer plants his seed, waters it, fertilizes it, but in the end he trusts that God will cause the seed to grow into a healthy crop. As an athlete, practice is like planting the seed for the farmer. You practice and practice, and may even get tired of simply practicing. But then when the game times comes and you need to execute a play, you are glad for all the practice you have put into it.

Do you ever get tired and weary of practicing over and over again? What do you do to keep yourself going?

_____

_____

_____

_____

_____

_____

_____

_____

_____

_____

_____

_____

_____

_____

Be Consistent in Practice

**By contrast, the boy Samuel grew in stature
and in favor with the Lord and with men.**

—1 Samuel 2:26

Do you or your parents chart how much you grow in height from year to year? Growing up I had a door in my garage and on every birthday my parents would measure my growth from year to year. If you measure it every day, you can't see the change. But change was happening every day; I just didn't see it until the yearly birthday check up. Be consistent in your time with the Lord and in your practice. Without realizing it, God is working and causing change in you, which is a very good thing.

Do you see that you are changing all the time? What are some changes you've noticed this year?

_____

_____

_____

_____

_____

_____

_____

_____

_____

_____

_____

_____

_____

_____

Don't Be Arrogant

**But as for me, my feet almost slipped;
my steps nearly went astray. For I envied
the arrogant; I saw the prosperity of the wicked.**

—Psalm 73:2–3

Who is your hero in your sport? How does she act on the field after she has made a great play? What do you know about her life outside of the game? Is her lifestyle one you would like to follow? Often the ones who succeed in sports are very cocky and arrogant about their success, giving all the glory to themselves for what they have done. It is easy to want to be like them. But God challenges us not to get caught up in the applause of women, but rather to play for Jesus who gives you the ability to play in the first place.

Do your heroes have a good reputation on and off the field or court? How is that important for you too?

_____

_____

_____

_____

_____

_____

_____

_____

_____

_____

_____

_____

_____

_____

Stand Firm in the Lord

**Be alert, stand firm in the faith,
act like a man, be strong.**

—1 Corinthians 16:13

Have you ever watched an oak tree withstand a thunderstorm with a mighty wind beating constantly on its limbs? It is amazing. It just keeps taking the beating and stands firm till after the storm. How is it able to withstand the storm? By digging its roots deep into the ground. Your roots are your relationship with the Lord. Spend time with Him daily by sharing your thoughts with Him and reading the Bible. Then when the storms of life come, you will find that you, like the oak tree, are able to stand firm and not lose faith.

How much time do you spend with the Lord? Do you have a daily routine? Are your roots deep?

_____

_____

_____

_____

_____

_____

_____

_____

_____

_____

_____

_____

_____

_____

Pride Goes Before Destruction

**Pride comes before destruction,
and an arrogant spirit before a fall.**

—Proverbs 16:18

Are you prideful? Pride can be a good thing but can also be a very bad thing. It is positive when we have pride in our country or our team, or in the way we keep our house cleaned. But it can quickly become negative when we feel superior or conceited or arrogant to others. This kind of pride is something that God despises greatly because it is taking what is God's (your God-given ability) and acting like you did it all on your own instead of with God's help. Keep humble in all you do, realizing that everything you have is a gift from God.

Are you prideful? How do you maintain a balance between good pride and bad pride? What is humility?

_____

_____

_____

_____

_____

_____

_____

_____

_____

_____

_____

_____

_____

_____

Rules Are for Our Protection

If anyone competes as an athlete, he is not crowned unless he competes according to the rules.

—2 Timothy 2:5

To win the game you have to play by the rules. If you try to get around the rules, the official's job is to keep you within the guidelines of the game and penalize you. The rules in a sporting event are to keep people safe and to keep the game fair. If every person could write his own rules, it would be bedlam. In life, God has given us rules as well. They are written in the Bible. One of the purposes of the Bible is to guide us through life, to give us rules to protect us and provide a straight path for us.

How do you react to rules? Are you a rule keeper? How does this reflect your relationship with God?

_____

_____

_____

_____

_____

_____

_____

_____

_____

_____

_____

_____

_____

_____

God's Renewed Strength

May you be strengthened with all power, according to His glorious might, for all endurance and patience, with joy.

—Colossians 1:11

Where does your strength come from? Does it come from God or from you? Many people live their lives on their own strength. They work and work and work like it is all up to them. Hopefully in the end they find they had enough strength to pass the test or win the game. It is exhausting because it is all up to them, not with the help of the Lord. But those who trust in the Lord call on His strength and His power to help them through each practice, each game, each day. They find a renewed strength that gives joy instead of an exhausting strength that drains them or all their energy.

Where does your strength come from? Does it come from God or from you? How do you get strength from God?

_____

_____

_____

_____

_____

_____

_____

_____

_____

_____

_____

_____

_____

_____

Ask for God's Strength

Do you not know? Have you not heard? Yahweh is the ever-lasting God, the Creator of the whole earth. He never grows faint or weary; there is no limit to His understanding.

—Isaiah 40:28

Some days the last thing you want to do is go to practice one more time. Yet you have to find the strength to go anyway. Where does this strength come from? Ask God to give you strength, and He will answer your prayers. He never grows tired or weary. His wisdom is beyond our understanding. Not only did He create us, He knows us so well and wants to be there for us to give us His strength.

God never gets tired, so can you get more energy from Him? Can He really give you strength?

_____

_____

_____

_____

_____

_____

_____

_____

_____

_____

_____

_____

_____

God Heals the Brokenhearted

He heals the brokenhearted and binds up their wounds.

—Psalm 147:3

Losing a close game can feel like it breaks your heart. You gave all you had and just came a little short on the scoreboard. Yet the above Scripture tells us that God knows your heart is broken and will put it back together. First of all He doesn't try to cover up or hide your pain. He knows it hurts to lose and acknowledges the pain. But then He comforts you in your pain and gives you the strength to make it through the next day, the next game, the next practice. He is the great healer. Run to Him.

Have you ever been brokenhearted? How did you get over it?

_____

_____

_____

_____

_____

_____

_____

_____

_____

_____

_____

_____

_____

_____

Be Slow to Speak

My dearly loved brothers, understand this: Everyone must be quick to hear, slow to speak, and slow to anger, for man's anger does not accomplish God's righteousness.

—James 1:19–20

Have you ever been at a game when a fan (usually a dad) yells out of control at the official? Sporting events bring out our emotions, good and bad. Often something will happen in the game and it makes your anger almost explode inside of you. You feel like if you don't let it out, you will explode. The Bible tells us to be slow to speak, especially when we are angry. Back away from the situation and give God your anger.

Have you ever lost your temper during the game? Has someone you know ever yelled at the official? What happened?

_____

_____

_____

_____

_____

_____

_____

_____

_____

_____

_____

_____

_____

_____

_____

God Is the Creator of All

Who has measured the waters in the hollow of his hand or marked off the heavens with the span of his hand? Who has gathered the dust of the earth in a measure or weighed the mountains in a balance and the hills in the scales?

—Isaiah 40:12

Where does the strength come from to finish the race? Many athletes live their lives and compete with the mind-set that it is all up to them to finish and succeed. With that mind-set, it is very easy to become arrogant or cocky because it is all about them. But the Bible tells us that God is the one who gives us power and strength. As our Creator, He is the one who gives us the strength to finish the race. Therefore we compete as hard as we can and we push our bodies as hard as we can, but we realize that God is the one who sees us through to the end.

Where does your strength come from to finish the race? Have you ever just quit because you were tired?

_____

_____

_____

_____

_____

_____

_____

_____

_____

_____

_____

_____

_____

_____

Encourage One Another

Fulfill my joy by thinking the same way, having the same love, sharing the same feelings, focusing on one goal.

—Philippians 2:2

How do you get along with your teammates? Your teammates have the potential of being some of the best friends in your life. Why? Because you are all committed to working for a common goal, making your team the best it can be. So you are giving your all and your teammates are giving their all, and in the process you find that there is a deep care for one another. You want to see them succeed and they want to see you succeed. Learn how to be a positive teammate who builds up her teammates instead of cutting them down.

Are your teammates your best friends? How do you get along with the members of your team?

_____

_____

_____

_____

_____

_____

_____

_____

_____

_____

_____

_____

_____

_____

_____

God's Power Never Leaves You

For David says of Him: I saw the Lord ever before me; because He is at my right hand, I will not be shaken.

—Acts 2:25

Where is God when you are competing in a game or practice? Do you feel like you are all alone as you are competing? Often when you are training and getting in shape you are alone. This passage tells us that even King David, the mighty king of Israel who had everyone looking to him to lead the nation, knew that the Lord was always with him. Therefore he knew that he would not be shaken. Realize God is with you every step of the way and go forth with His power.

Do you feel like you are all alone as you are competing?
What can you do to help you realize you aren't alone?

_____

_____

_____

_____

_____

_____

_____

_____

_____

_____

_____

_____

_____

_____

_____

_____

Pray at All Times

**Pray at all times in the Spirit with every
prayer and request, and stay alert in this with
all perseverance and intercession for all the saints.**

—Ephesians 6:18

What do you pray for during your game or practice? Prayer is simply talking with God about anything and everything. Prayer can happen anytime and anywhere. Pray to God for wisdom and strength as you practice. Pray to Him during games for the same thing. Pray to Him about your teammates and opponents. Pray in victories and defeats, in successes and failures. Pray at all times!

What do you pray for during your game or practice? Do you think God cares about your game? Why?

_____

_____

_____

_____

_____

_____

_____

_____

_____

_____

_____

_____

_____

_____

_____

_____

Don't Worry

**Can any of you add a single cubit
to his height by worrying?**

—Matthew 6:27

What do you worry about? Does worrying cause you to
play or practice better? Does worrying build you up or
tear you down? Worry usually causes you to tighten up
and not play as well. Give your worries to God and experience His peace in its place. When you start getting anxious about your game, simply turn it into a prayer request
to God. He cares for you and knows all about you. He
knows exactly what you need and when you need it.

Are you a worrier? What do you worry about? Does it help? How can you stop worrying?

_____

_____

_____

_____

_____

_____

_____

_____

_____

_____

_____

_____

_____

_____

Pay Day Is Coming!

**But as for you, be strong; don't be discouraged,
for your work has a reward.**

—2 Chronicles 15:7

For your parents, pay day is a great day. They receive
money for the work they have done. Every pay day there
is a sense of relief because they are getting paid for work
they have already done. In sports, "pay day" is often the
games. When you work hard in practice, games should
be a pay back for all the hard work you did in practice.
Sometimes knowing there is a pay day coming, a game
day, makes it much easier to make it through some tough
practices.

How do you get paid for your work? Do you feel like it's pay day when you win a game? Why?

_____

_____

_____

_____

_____

_____

_____

_____

_____

_____

_____

_____

_____

_____

Be Prepared!

Put on the full armor of God so that you can stand against the tactics of the Devil.

—Ephesians 6:11

What kind of equipment do you wear for your game? In softball, a catcher wears a chest guard, a mask, and shin guards. Each piece of equipment is designed to protect you from injury. In the Bible it gives a list of "equipment" for a Christian to put on to be able to protect yourself from the enemy. Prepare yourself spiritually just like you would prepare yourself physically for your contest.

What type of equipment do you need for your sport? How does that relate to your spiritual equipment?

_____

_____

_____

_____

_____

_____

_____

_____

_____

_____

_____

_____

_____

_____

_____

Feel the Emotions

Jesus wept.

—John 11:35

Think about the last time you cried. What emotions triggered the tears? Sometimes you cry because you are extremely sad because something bad happened. You may have lost a game or had an injury. But sometimes you may cry because you are so happy. Jesus wept here because His very good friend, Lazarus, died. He saw how upset his sisters Mary and Martha were. Even though He raised Lazarus from the dead a few minutes later, He still was in touch with the pain involved in Lazarus's death. Appreciate the emotions that the game brings.

What makes you cry? What is your attitude toward those who cry?

_____

_____

_____

_____

_____

_____

_____

_____

_____

_____

_____

_____

_____

_____

_____

Play for God!

Whatever you do, do it enthusiastically, as something done for the Lord and not for men.

—Colossians 3:23

How do you work heartily? How do you practice heartily and play heartily? Do you play for your parents, your coach, the fans, or do you play for the Lord? God doesn't really care what you do, but He does care greatly about how you do what you do. He created you with the ability to give Him your all every time you go out. Go full speed and give every ounce of strength you have to your sport. Play in a way that makes God smile and don't worry about what the world says.

In your sport, what opportunities do you have to honor God by the way you play? Who do you play for?

_____

_____

_____

_____

_____

_____

_____

_____

_____

_____

_____

_____

_____

_____

Be a Friend to Your Teammates

**A friend loves at all times, and a brother
is born for a difficult time.**

—Proverbs 17:17

Great friendships are developed through sporting events. Some of the closest friends in the world may very well be your teammates. Why? One reason is because you both love the same sport. Learn how to encourage your teammates. Enjoy sweating beside them in practice and being on the same team with them. Pour out your heart to them. Tell them what you like about the sport. Tell them when it is hard. Give them a high five when they succeed. Be there for them when they might not measure up and fail. Be a true friend to them on and off the field.

How can you be a better teammate? What are some ways you can encourage those who don't always play well?

_____

_____

_____

_____

_____

_____

_____

_____

_____

_____

_____

_____

_____

_____

_____

Make a Difference for Christ's Sake

But I count my life of no value to myself, so that I may finish my course and the ministry I received from the Lord Jesus, to testify to the gospel of God's grace.

—Acts 20:24

Do you realize that you have the awesome opportunity to make a difference on your team for Christ's sake? You can show other people who Jesus is not just in your words but even more so by your actions. You have the opportunity to show other people (teammates and opponents) what a relationship with Jesus is all about. They will notice how hard you practice, what you say when things don't go right, how you handle defeat, and how you handle victory. Make a difference in this world for Christ's sake.

Do you realize that you have the awesome opportunity to make a difference on your team for Christ's sake? How?

_____

_____

_____

_____

_____

_____

_____

_____

_____

_____

_____

_____

_____

_____

Bring Words of Encouragement

No foul language is to come from your mouth, but only what is good for building up someone in need, so that it gives grace to those who hear.

—Ephesians 4:29

What you say matters. The words that come out of your mouth can either build up your teammates or tear them down. Sometimes when your team is down because things are not going well in the game, it takes the words of a teammate to pick up the team and encourage them to keep trying and trying. When the team sees you encouraging them and never losing heart, it will strengthen them to do the same. Learn when to speak up with words of encouragement and learn when to be silent.

How do your team members encourage one another and build each other up?

_____

_____

_____

_____

_____

_____

_____

_____

_____

_____

_____

_____

_____

Honor Your Opponents

**Do not take revenge or bear a grudge
against members of your community, but love
your neighbor as yourself; I am Yahweh.**

—Leviticus 19:18

How do you treat your opponents? It is very easy to look
down on your opponents and try to destroy them. Beating
them on the scoreboard is one thing and really is one of
the reasons you play the game. But how you treat your
opponent during and after the game is a very important
part of life. Try as hard as you can to defeat your opponent, but do so with all respect and honor. If they make
a good play on you, congratulate them. Treat your opponent the way you would like to be treated, for the Lord is
Lord of both of you.

How do you treat your opponents? Is there respect and kindness or rude behavior?

_____

_____

_____

_____

_____

_____

_____

_____

_____

_____

_____

_____

_____

_____

_____

Give Your All

**Make yourself an example of good works
with integrity and dignity in your teaching.**

—Titus 2:7

What is your work ethic like? Do you practice as hard as you play? Do you give everything you have in every game on every play? Have you ever wondered why professional football players have to be taken out of the game so often? Why can't an offensive player also play defense? It is because they give every ounce of their strength on every play and their bodies must have rest. Learn to give wholeheartedly to your practice and games, and be a model for others to see.

What is your work ethic like? Do you give everything you have in every game on every play?

_____

_____

_____

_____

_____

_____

_____

_____

_____

_____

_____

_____

_____

God's Peace

**Peace I leave with you. My peace I give to you.
I do not give to you as the world gives.
Your heart must not be troubled or fearful.**

—John 14:27

What kind of peace does the world give? According to the world peace only comes when you win. There is no second place, only first. But the peace that God gives isn't based on the scoreboard. It is based on you giving your best effort and loving your teammates with all your heart. That peace lasts much longer than a worldly peace that fades away shortly after the game is over.

Why are you playing sports? Do you enjoy it and have fun? How can God's peace work through you?

_____

_____

_____

_____

_____

_____

_____

_____

_____

_____

_____

_____

_____

_____